Presented to:

James Beaumont

Ladybank Gospel Hall
Youth Club 2015-2016

50 GOOD BIBLE STORIES

50 GORIEST BIBLE STORIES

Andy Robb

CWR

Published 2009 by CWR, Waverley Abbey House, Waverley Lane, Farnham, Surrey GU9 8EP, UK. Registered Charity No. 294387. Registered Limited Company No. 1990308. Reprinted 2010, 2012, 2014.

See back of book for list of National Distributors.

Editing, design and production by CWR

Cover image: Andy Robb

Printed in England by Linney Print

ISBN: 978-1-85345-530-8

Intro

Congratulations!

Buying this book is one of the smartest decisions you'll ever make if you're wanting to get your teeth into the Bible but aren't quite sure where to start. Not only have we hand-picked some of the best bits for you, but we've also chopped them up into nice, easy-to-chomp morsels. How's that for thoughtfulness?

In this tasty book we've served up fifty juicy, bite-sized bits of the Bible to munch on and loads of crazy cartoon pics to make them easy for you to digest.

To keep you on your toes, we've mixed up the Old and New Testament stories. Not sure what the difference is between them? It's simple. New Testament stories kick off from when Jesus showed up on planet Earth. The Old Testament happened before that and goes right back to the beginning of time.

But if you're thinking that this book

is all about being spoon-fed stuff from the Bible so that you don't have to lift a finger, think again! At the end of each Bible bit there's some investigating work for you to do, which means you'll need to get your hands on a Bible if you want to find out how the stories end.

Just in case you've bought this book but you don't know much about the Bible, let me give you some useful facts …

Fact number one:
Although the Bible is one book (and what a whopper it is), it's actually made up of sixty-six mini books.

Fact number two:
The Bible wasn't written by just one person like most books. It has over forty authors.

Fact number three:
The Bible was written over a period of roughly 1,500 years.

Fact number four:
Everything that's in the Bible was God's idea.

Next up, you're gonna need to know how to read the Bible – and I don't mean from left to right and top to bottom.

The first thing to know is that every Bible book has got its own name, such as Joshua, Judges, Job, Jeremiah, Joel, Jonah,

John, James or Jude. To make these Bible books easier to read, they're handily divided up into chapters (like normal books) and then each chapter is broken up into verses (like you get in poems). All clear so far? Good!

So, if you wanted to check out Bible book Genesis, chapter 5 and verses 25 to 27, here's how it's often written down:

Genesis 5:25-27

Check out these verses and you'll discover who the world's oldest man was (ever) and how many birthday cards he would have received if they'd been invented way back then (which they hadn't).

That's about it.

So what are you waiting for? Tuck in!

1
BELLY TUBBY

The Moabites had been giving the Israelites a hard time for the past eighteen years, and the Israelites had done their usual and begged God to help. So God gave them a leader called Ehud who decided to do something about those monstrous Moabites. Just for your info, Ehud was left-handed. Nothing odd about that, you may say, and you'd be right. But read on and find out how being left-handed caught Ehud's enemy by surprise.

The Israelites packed Ehud off for a head to head with King Eglon of Moab. Being a generous sort of chap, Ehud went bearing gifts for the king. For good measure, he also tucked a half-metre long, double-edged sword under his clothes. Ehud delivered his goodies to King Eglon and then made out as if he was leaving. But this was all part of his plan. He sent home the men who'd come along to carry the gifts and then went back to see the king one more time.

Crafty Ehud pretended he had a secret message for Eglon, so the unsuspecting king booted all of his servants out and the pair were left alone. Oh yes, there's one thing I should have told you about our Moabite king. How can I say this tactfully? Er, well actually, I can't. I'll come straight out with it. He was a

fatty. Sorry, but that's the truth of it.

As Ehud leaned over to pretend to deliver his message to the king, Eglon stood to his feet. With his left hand, Israel's leader plunged his sharp sword into the Moabite king's bulbous, blubbery belly. Now here's where the left-handed bit comes in. In those days, most people wielded their weapons in their right hand, so King Eglon wouldn't have suspected a thing when Ehud slipped his left hand under his tunic to whip out the sword. Nice one, Ehud!

If you want to find out what became of Ehud's sword, then check out Bible book Judges, chapter 3 and verses 22 through to 25.

JUDE THE DOUBLE-CROSSING DUDE

If you know anything about Jesus then you've probably heard of a guy called Judas Iscariot, one of His disciples. Things started to go from bad to worse for Judas when a lady poured a jar of top-of-the-range perfume over Jesus to honour Him. Judas was livid. What a complete waste of money – well, at least that's what Judas thought. Who knows why he eventually gave up on Jesus, but something snapped inside him and he decided enough was enough. He simply couldn't be one of Jesus' followers any longer.

Judas was well aware that the religious leaders in Israel were champing at the bit to get rid of Jesus. He was always challenging their way of doing things and winning hands down when it came to popularity with the crowds. They must have rubbed their hands with glee when Judas approached them with the offer of betraying Jesus into their hands. It was a done deal. Thirty pieces of silver in exchange for Judas leading them to a secluded place to arrest Jesus, far away from all those adoring crowds. But Jesus was under no illusions where Judas' loyalties stood. During His last meal with His disciples, He sent shock waves through the room when He predicted that one of them would betray Him.

Sure enough, that night, Jesus and the other eleven disciples were out on a hillside around Jerusalem when Judas turned up with a posse of religious leaders and an armed mob. He did the dirty deed and identified Jesus with a kiss. The religious leaders were over the moon. They finally had their man.

Throughout the night Jesus was cross-examined and then handed over to the Roman governor. Judas realised he'd made a big mistake and tried to get the religious leaders to change their minds. But they'd got what they wanted and tough luck if Judas was now having his conscience pricked. Judas threw the thirty coins into the Temple and went off and hanged himself. He couldn't live with the horror of what he'd done.

If you want an even gorier version of Judas' death then head for Bible book Acts, chapter 1 and verses 18 and 19.

3
OX BOX

The secret to the Israelites' success was God being with them. And there was nothing that better represented God being slap bang in the middle of everything they did than a small, rectangular box called the ark of the covenant. Inside this rather ornate box were two slabs of stone (with the ten commandments chiselled onto them), a golden pot of manna (a miraculous food that fed the Israelites for forty years) and a wooden walking stick that God caused to bloom. The bottom line is that the Israelites had made a bit of a hash of looking after the ark and it wasn't in God's Temple in Jerusalem where it should have been.

Israel now had a new king, David, and top of his 'must do' list was retrieving the ark from a guy called Abinadab who'd been taking care of it for the past twenty years. Not being one to do things by halves, David headed off to Abinadab's place (in Baalah), with 30,000 of his crack troops in tow, to collect the box and return it to Jerusalem. Now, there's something you should know about the ark of the covenant. Because it was so special, God had instructed the Israelites the precise way to transport it from A to B. The job of lugging it around was the privilege of a select bunch of Israelites called priests

and they had to carry it on shoulder poles. Woe betide anyone who chose to do it differently! But listen to how King David went and moved the box.

Perhaps he was having an off day and wasn't thinking straight. Anyway he completely ignored God's instructions and just plopped the ark onto an ox cart, and headed back to Jerusalem. One of Abinadab's boys, Uzzah, was in charge of steering the cart, and the Israelites were whooping it up, jigging about and making a right old din with their cymbals, lyres, harps, rattles and drums. Just when the carnival atmosphere was reaching fever pitch, disaster struck. One of the oxen pulling the cart stumbled. Without thinking, Uzzah grabbed the box to stop it from falling.

Whoops! Big mistake. Zap! God killed Uzzah right where he stood because of his lack of reverence.

To find out what happened next in this gory story you're going to have to check out Bible book 2 Samuel, chapter 6 and verses 9 to 11.

4

BLOOD BROTHERS

Imagine having Adam and Eve (the world's first two people) as your parents. Well, that was what it was like for a guy called Cain and his kid brother, Abel. Adam and Eve had been specially handmade by God but their kids were born in the usual way (like the rest of us).

When they'd grown up, the brothers did what most people do and got themselves a job. Cain opted for becoming a farmer and Abel became a shepherd. In time, the pair both decided to show their appreciation to God by bringing Him a gift. How thoughtful! Cain showed up with some of the stuff he'd been growing in his fields and Abel brought God the first lamb born to one of his sheep. Was God bowled over by their gratitude? Well, yes and no. Abel was spot on with his animal offering but Cain was wide of the mark with his harvest goodies.

Although the Bible doesn't quite spell it out in so many words, it's pretty obvious that both of them were well aware what sort of offerings were acceptable to God, and Cain seems to have completely ignored this.

As far as God was concerned, this couldn't-care-less attitude revealed what a bad lad Cain really was. To prove the point, Cain went ballistic when God turned His nose up at his crop

offering. God tried to calm Cain down but he was having none of it. He was mad, mad, mad and could only think of one thing … revenge! Hiding his fury for a moment, Cain calmly invited Abel out into the fields. If Abel had figured that there were no hard feelings between him and Cain then he had another thing coming. As soon as they were out in the countryside, Cain let rip and killed his younger brother.

God saw it all and gave Cain the chance to come clean. 'Where is your brother Abel?' God already knew the answer but Cain added insult to injury and brazenly lied that he hadn't a clue. 'Am I my brother's keeper?' God wasn't fooled and told Cain that his wickedness was going to be punished.

Head for Bible book Genesis, chapter 4 and read verses 11 through to 16 to discover precisely how.

5
THE STAY AFLOAT BOAT

Things weren't looking too good on planet Earth. When God created the world (and everything in it) there wasn't a bad bit to be found. But before you could say, 'Thanks, God, but I think we can manage without You', the hearts of most people had turned bad. They'd become so wicked that God was wishing He'd never made humans in the first place.

God made up His mind to wipe people off the face of the earth, with the exception of a guy called Noah. Noah wasn't like the rest and the Bible tells us that God was pleased with him. God's plan was to send a ginormous flood that would clear away all of the grot. That meant that Noah (and his family) needed some sort of protection from the destruction heading their way. How about a boat? They're quite handy when it comes to avoiding being drowned. Sounds good!

God had the same thought and gave our main man (Noah) detailed instructions on how to build a whopper of a vessel that was not only going to be big enough to hold him, his wife, his three lads and *their* wives, but also a male and female

of every living creature. If the world was going to be repopulated after the flood then it was pretty important that there should be creatures to live on it. Just for your info, the boat (or ark as it was also called) was 437 feet long, 44 feet high, had three decks and room for 432 double decker buses inside (if they'd been invented, which they hadn't). Noah's neighbours must have thought the four of them were off their heads making a boat miles from the nearest ocean. When the flood came I'll bet they changed their tune.

Once the animals were loaded on board and Noah and his family were safe inside, the skies opened and it bucketed down. God also opened up all the underground reservoirs to make sure that absolutely nothing escaped the deluge. The Bible helpfully informs us that Noah was 600 years old when the flood began and it kept on chucking it down for forty days.

The gory truth is that every living being on the earth was destroyed: humans, animals, birds. You name it, the flood killed it.

Just in case you're worried that God might do the same again one day, check out Bible book Genesis, chapter 9 and verses 8 to 17 for a bit of reassurance.

6
THAT'S YOUR LOT!

If you've heard of a fella called Abraham then there's a good chance you've also heard of his nephew, Lot. This Bible story tells us a lot about Lot and a lot about how he tried to please God – a lot.

Lot lived in a place called Sodom which, to be perfectly honest, was not a nice place for a good guy like Lot to be hanging out in. Sodom was full of wicked people, and when a couple of God's angels showed up things went from bad to worse.

It wasn't safe to be out at night in that city so Lot persuaded the angels to spend the night at his place. When the mean men of Sodom found out about Lot's visitors, they surrounded the house and told Lot to send them outside. They were meaning to harm them but Lot was desperate to protect his special guests. Just as the wicked men of Sodom were lining themselves up to batter down the door to Lot's house, the angels sprang into action and struck the attackers with blindness.

While the men groped around in the darkness, the angels gave Lot his marching orders to leave the city, pronto! God was planning to wipe Sodom (and the equally wicked nearby town of Gomorrah) off the face of the earth. There was not a moment to lose. Lot and his family needed to beat it as fast as their legs could carry them.

Not everyone was convinced by Lot's frantic pleas to run for the hills, but time was running out. The angels grabbed Lot, his wife and his two daughters and sped them out of the city. Dawn was breaking and God was about to wreak havoc in that vile valley. As they ran for their lives, burning sulphur rained down from the sky destroying Sodom and Gomorrah completely.

All of a sudden, Lot's wife had second thoughts about leaving. A quick flick through your Bible to Genesis, chapter 19 and verse 26 will reveal her fate.

TESTING TIMES

Don't tell me, I bet you think that your parents are ancient. You do, don't you? Thought so! Well, spare a thought for poor Isaac. His dad (Abraham) was 100 years old when he was born and his mum (Sarah) wasn't far behind. Try explaining that one away to your mates.

Isaac was a bit of a special kid and God had promised Abraham that through Isaac, he'd have as many descendants as there are stars in the sky – which is an awful lot.

Just when everything seemed to be going well God dropped a massive bombshell. He told Abraham to head for the mountains and to sacrifice his one and only son to Him. Surely He couldn't mean Isaac. There must be some mistake. Nope! Abraham heard right. So, with a couple of servants in tow (and not forgetting Isaac, of course) he loaded up his donkey with wood for the sacrifice and set off to do the deed. After a three-day trek they arrived at Mount Moriah. Abraham left his servants to take care of the donkey and climbed the mountain with Isaac.

It suddenly crossed Isaac's mind that they had stuff with which to burn the sacrifice but no actual sacrifice. Abraham blagged his way out of telling his lad that *he* was going to be

the sacrifice by saying that God would sort it. At the spot
God had told him, Abraham built an altar and arranged the
wood on it. That was when the rubber hit the road. Abraham
tied up Isaac and laid him on top of the wood pile. It was
probably at this point that Isaac started to panic. Whether
Abraham panicked as well is anyone's guess but he obediently
picked up a sharp knife and got ready to kill his son.

Just in the nick of time, an angel from God yelled down
from heaven at the top of his voice, 'Don't hurt the boy!' Phew,
that was a close shave. God had never intended for Abraham
to end Isaac's life. He was simply testing him to see how much
he trusted and honoured
God. He'd passed
with flying
colours.

So, did Abraham sacrifice anything
else to God in place of Isaac?
Take a look at Bible book Genesis,
chapter 22 and verse 13.

CROC SHOCK

Some background info. A small group of Israelites had emigrated to Egypt (because of a famine in their land) but as time passed, their numbers grew until there were so many of them that Egypt's king (Pharaoh) started to feel a wee bit threatened. Pharaoh hit upon a dastardly plan to stop things in their tracks. He sent for Shiphrah and Puah (the Israelites' midwives) and ordered them to kill every Israelite baby boy that was born. He figured that that oughta slow down population growth a bit.

The good news is that Shiphrah and Puah feared God a lot more than they feared Egypt's horrid king. The brave midwives completely ignored the king's cunning command and came up with an excellent excuse: the Israelite baby boys were born so quickly that it was all over before they arrived. Nice one, ladies!

The king was not a happy bunny. There seemed to be no stopping these Israelites. At the rate they were going they'd outnumber the Egyptians in no time at all and that simply wouldn't do.

Egypt's king decided to take matters into his own hands and decreed that every newborn Israelite boy was to be flung

into the River Nile. Didn't he know that the Nile was full of crocodiles? Yep, he sure did. Gory or what!

Not every baby copped it. One mum hid her kid for three months until she couldn't keep him secret any longer. She put her son in a watertight basket and placed him in the tall grass at the edge of the Nile. Who should be passing but the king's daughter, out by the river to take a dip. Did she chuck the Israelite boy into the River Nile so that he went the way of all the other babies?

Head for Bible book Exodus, chapter 2 and check out verses 5 to 10 for your answer.

9
GO JOE!

nless you've been living on Planet Zog all your life then you'll know all about Joseph and his splendid coloured coat. Joseph was the apple of his dad's eye which didn't go down too well with the rest of his brothers (all eleven of them). They'd had enough of Joseph the blue-eyed boy and his dreams of one day ruling over them. Joseph needed pulling down a peg or two and it was time he got his come-uppance.

The brothers were out and about looking after their dad's flocks. Jacob (their dad) dispatched Joe to go and check that they were getting on all right. As Joseph approached them they hatched a plot to kill him, throw his body into a well and make out it had been the work of wild animals. Isn't brotherly love a wonderful thing? Reuben (the eldest) wasn't so keen on the plan and tried to save Joe's life by suggesting that they leave out the killing bit and just throw him down a well. (Reuben's idea was to rescue Joseph later.) Yep, they could run with that, or at least that's what they said to Reuben.

When Joseph arrived, they ripped off the long sleeved, coloured coat his dad had made for him and flung their upstart brother into the well (which, fortunately for Joe, was dry at the time). With the dirty deed done, they put their feet

up and tucked into their packed lunch.

Very soon a bunch of Ishmaelite traders passed by on
their way to Egypt. One of the brothers (Judah) began to
have second thoughts about killing Joseph. He had a better
idea. How about selling him as a slave to the Ishmaelites? If
they took Joseph to far away Egypt he'd be out of their hair
forever. So that's what they did. The brothers sold him for
twenty pieces of silver and then went back to their
dad and spun a gory
yarn about what had
befallen their poor
brother, Joe.

Read the pack of lies they told
Jacob in Bible book Genesis,
chapter 37 and from verse 31
through to verse 35.

YOU'RE FIRED!

This Bible story might be a bit short but take it from me, it's hot stuff!

It stars (very briefly) Nahab and Abihu. Their claim to fame (other than making a guest appearance in the Bible) was having Moses – I'm sure you've heard of him – as their uncle. Their dad, Aaron, was also quite well known. He was Moses' brother and his job was as Israel's high priest.

Aaron was in charge of the sacrifices that were presented to God in the tabernacle (a special tent where God showed up in all his splendour). This wasn't a job any old Tom, Dick or Harry could do. Priests had to belong to Israel's Levite tribe and had a long list of 'dos' and 'don'ts' to make sure they performed their duties in the way God wanted.

Although God is full of love, He's also holy and awesome which means you don't mess with Him, as Aaron's boys were about to find out. Aaron had just finished a stint in the tabernacle and now it was the turn of Nahab and Abihu. Each of them took a pan of hot, fiery coals, added incense to it and presented it to God. Was God pleased with their offering? Well, not according to the Bible. It says that God hadn't told them to do that and on top of that the fire wasn't even holy.

Okay, so that doesn't explain a lot but take it from me, God knows what He's talking about. If God says that Nadab and Abihu were out of line with Him then they must have been, end of story! The bottom line is that Aaron's sons must have been doing something really bad and God wasn't pleased. Without a word of warning, He sent down some fire of His own and burnt the pair to a frazzle because of their lack of respect for Him.

Find out what happened to Nadab and Abihu's barbecued bodies, and also what God told their dad to do in Bible book Leviticus, chapter 10 and verses 4 to 7.

TREBLE TROUBLE

God had handpicked Moses to lead the Israelites out from slavery in Egypt but not everyone was so keen on the idea of him being the main man. Three guys called Korah, Dathan and Abiram thought that Moses was getting a bit too big for his boots and they wanted a say in how things were run. Moses was horrified and prayed to God about the rumpus. He tried to convince these rebels that complaining against God's leaders (him) was the same as complaining about God and that was a mighty mistake. There was nothing for it but to prove to this troublesome trio, once and for all, who was in charge. A meeting was arranged for the next day and Moses told Korah to bring all his followers (250 in total) with him. It was showdown time.

As they stood outside the tabernacle tent (where sacrifices were made to God) God showed up in all His dazzling power. Moses got the nod from God to stand clear. He was going to wipe this bunch of rebels off the face of the earth. But first, before He struck them down, He had some other scores to settle. God allowed Moses to clear the area around Korah and his two accomplices' tents of innocent bystanders. Dathan and Abiram (along with their wives and kids) came out of their

tents to see what all the commotion was. Then God sprang
into action to show that it was a mistake to challenge the
leadership of His man, Moses. The ground split beneath them
and swallowed up every last man, woman and child of Korah,
Dathan and Abiram's families. Along with all their worldly
wealth, they were buried alive and then the
ground closed over
them. And
that was that.

What became of Korah and his
250 followers who were standing
outside the tabernacle tent? Did
they escape scot-free? Look up
Bible book Numbers, chapter 16
and verse 35 to discover all.

12 WALL FALL

Here's a story I reckon you'll know. There was this guy called Joshua who was gearing up to conquer the land of Canaan so that his people (the Israelites) could set up home there. Joshua's battle plan was to take the land, bit by bit, and the first place on his hit list was the walled city of Jericho. Because this was all God's idea, Joshua wasn't allowed to attack Jericho as he pleased. God wanted it done His way so that He got the credit. God's rather unconventional plan of attack was for Joshua and his army to march around the city, once a day for six days. Heading up the procession were gonna be the priests carrying the ark of the covenant (a special box) with some of them blowing trumpets. That was it! No attacking. No fighting. Just six laps of Jericho.

Hmm, sounds a bit odd. But not to Joshua. He'd spent long enough hanging around God to know better than to argue with this bizarre strategy. He followed God's instructions to the letter, day after day, until day seven arrived. I'll bet the people of Jericho were scratching their heads wondering what on earth the Israelites were up to. They didn't have long to wait to find out.

On the seventh day, God had told Joshua to do the same thing again only this time it wasn't one lap of the city they had to march, but seven. With the seven circuits of the city completed, the priests blew their trumpets and Joshua gave orders for his men to shout because God had given the city into their hands.

You'll have to find out what happened next by taking a look at Bible book Joshua, chapter 6 and verses 20 to 21.

13
TENTS HEADACHE

The Israelites had been conquered by King Jabin of Canaan because they'd turned their backs on God. Jabin was a bit of a meanie and the Israelites cried out to God to rescue them from his clutches. One of Israel's leaders (Deborah) got a message from God to tell a guy called Barak to go to war against Sisera, the commander of Jabin's army.

God promised that He'd give Barak's 10,000 strong army the victory over their enemy, which was kind of reassuring, wasn't it?

Barak was a bit of a wuss and wouldn't go into battle without Deborah by his side. Deborah reluctantly agreed to go with him but said that he wouldn't get any credit for winning the battle. God would also hand Sisera over to a woman.

So the two armies came head to head, but God threw Sisera's army into confusion and, just as He said, God gave the Israelites the victory.

The Israelites killed the lot of 'em. Not a man was left alive, except that is for Sisera. He'd scarpered and hot-footed it to the tent of a fella called Heber who was at peace with King Jabin. Heber's missus (Jael) welcomed the exhausted Canaanite commander into their tent and hid him behind a curtain. Then Sisera asked the hostess with mostess to stand guard to make sure nobody discovered his whereabouts.

He was so flaked out from the events of the day that in no time at all he was sleeping like a baby. Heber's helpful wife rounded off her hospitality by tiptoeing up to the comatose commander and driving a tent peg through the side of his head with a hammer. Messy!

Was Jael embarrassed about her gory handiwork? A glance at Bible book Judges, chapter 4 and verse 22 will tell all.

FOOLED YA!

Joshua's army had just conquered the Canaanite city of Jericho and they were now setting their sights on a place called Ai. This time God had a different strategy. Here's how it went.

First Joshua dispatched a detachment of soldiers to hide at the back of the city. Once they were in place, Joshua and the rest of his troops made out as if they were lining themselves up to attack Ai from the front.

The king of Ai soon spotted them and mustered his fighting men to attack the Israelites. This was where the fun started – well, it did for Joshua and his army.

Joshua and his soldiers, pretending to run for their lives, began to retreat, pursued by Ai's A1 army. There wasn't a man left in the city as they chased after Joshua and his men. God then told Joshua to point his spear towards Ai. It was a sign to Joshua that the city was his for the taking. As soon as he did this, the men who Joshua had left in hiding ran into the city (which had been left wide open) and captured it. They torched the place and when the men of Ai looked back and saw smoke rising they realised that they'd been well and

truly outsmarted. Joshua's army had them surrounded with no means of escape. The Israelites slaughtered every one of them including every inhabitant of Ai. All 12,000! Only one person survived being skewered by the sword.

To find out who that was and whether he had a lucky escape check out Bible book Joshua, chapter 8 and verses 28 and 29.

PLUNDER BLUNDER

When the Israelites conquered the city of Jericho God had told them not to take any of the plunder for themselves. Any gold, silver, bronze and iron was to be taken and put into Israel's treasury; everything else was to be utterly destroyed. As you're about to find out, obedience to Him is something God expects.

The first attempt Joshua (Israel's leader) made to conquer the city of Ai ended in disaster. His small army was beaten something rotten by the men of Ai and was forced to retreat. Joshua was mortified. Wasn't God supposed to be with them in battle? Once word got out about their defeat they'd be pummelled by every nation around them. Joshua and the leaders of Israel threw themselves on the ground in despair. How on earth were they going to conquer the land of Canaan (which God had told them was theirs for the taking) at this rate?

God soon put a stop to their pity party and informed Joshua that the reason for their defeat was that someone had brought back into their camp the spoils of war from Jericho. The disobedience of one man was the root cause of their trouble, end of story. Much to Joshua's relief God told him that He was going to expose the culprit.

The next morning Joshua assembled the Israelites and started to work his way through them, tribe by tribe. First up was the tribe of Judah. They came forward, one clan at a time. When the clan of Zerah presented themselves, the family of Zabdi was picked out. From Zabdi's clan, Achan (Zabdi's grandson) was singled out. Joshua grilled Achan until he finally admitted that he'd nicked a Babylonian cloak, some silver and some gold.

The game was up. Achan had been rumbled and he spilled the beans and confessed that the goodies were buried inside his tent. Joshua's men went to find out if Achan was telling the truth. He was. Did Achan get let off the hook for owning up to his crime?

You'll find out all you need to know in Bible book Joshua, chapter 7 and verses 24 to 26.

VILE NILE

The king of Egypt (also known as Pharaoh) was being a stubborn so-and-so. The Israelites had been held captive as slaves in his country for hundreds of years and when a guy called Moses showed up and told the king that God wanted the lot of 'em released, he was well miffed. No way was he going to let his freebee work force just up and leave. I mean, how was he going to finish all the fabulous building projects on the cheap without his Israelite slaves. Little did he know that you don't mess with God.

God had given Moses' brother (Aaron) a wooden staff to perform miracles with so that Pharaoh would know who was boss. God told Moses and Aaron to rendezvous with the king down by the banks of the River Nile. When Pharaoh turned up Moses reminded him that God wanted the Israelites to go free, but because the king had refused to do what God commanded He was going to send a gory plague as a punishment.

Aaron lifted his wooden staff over all the rivers, canals and pools in Egypt. Before their very eyes the water turned to blood. Ugh! It was disgusting. Almost every drop of water in the land become blood.

Then Aaron struck the Nile itself and the same thing happened.

The river turned blood red and all its fish died. It stank something rotten and nobody could drink from it. Stiff-necked Pharaoh's magicians managed to use their magic to mimic the miracle, which made Pharoah even more determined to ignore God. Nevertheless the Egyptians spent seven thirsty days scavenging for water until God lifted the plague.

If you think that's a gory story then fast forward a few pages in Bible book Exodus, chapter 12 and check out verses 29 to 32 for God's final plague.

CAVE GRAVE

Joshua and the Israelites were working their way through the land of Canaan, conquering it bit by bit. The Gibeonites had tricked Joshua into signing a peace treaty with them, which didn't go down too well with King Adonizedek of Jerusalem who was still on Joshua's hit list. As far as Adonizedek was concerned, the Gibeonites had sold out to Israel and they deserved a good old thumping for turning traitor. The king of Jerusalem persuaded five Amorite kings to join forces with him and to attack scaredy-cat Gibeon.

When Joshua got wind of what was happening he headed off to rescue the Gibeonites with his tiptop troops. The Israelite army caught the Amorites by surprise and set about slaughtering the lot of them except, that is, for the five kings. They'd done a runner and were hiding out of harm's way (or so they thought) in a cave. But somebody rumbled them and snitched to Joshua.

Joshua ordered the entrance of the cave to be sealed with some big stones while they finished off the job of killing the Amorite army. Job done, Joshua had the quivering kings brought before him to discover their fate. Would he let them off?

Read the gory ending to this story in Bible book Joshua, chapter 10 and verses 26 and 27.

18 BULLSEYE!

The clash between David and Goliath is one of the most well known stories in the Bible, but its gory ending doesn't usually feature in most kids' books. Fear not, it does in this one!

Goliath was the Philistine army's star player and at around nine feet tall he scared the pants off their Israelite enemies. The Israelites and the Philistines were lined up for battle but it was a stalemate. King Saul (of Israel) couldn't find anyone to stand up to gargantuan Goliath. Goliath was having a field day and for forty frightening days he taunted the petrified Israelites, challenging them to send a man to fight him.

One day, a young guy called David showed up to deliver his brothers' packed lunch. When shepherd-boy David found out that Goliath was making the Israelites look like a bunch of wimps, he offered to go and fight the Philistine champion himself. Making mincemeat of that bully was nothing for someone like him who'd killed lions and bears while he'd been out looking after his dad's flocks. With God's help Goliath would be history.

David managed to persuade King Saul to let him have a shot at defeating the fearsome Philistine. The king reluctantly

agreed to the young lad's wild request. To be honest he had nothing to lose. Nobody else was in the queue for the job so it was David or nothing. David got kitted out in the king's armour but it was far too heavy for him. If he was going slay Goliath it would have to be in his normal clothes.

David bent down and picked up five smooth stones from a stream and, catapult at the ready, went out to meet Goliath. Goliath couldn't believe his eyes. Was this lad the best the Israelites could come up with? They had to be kidding.

David ignored Goliath's mocking comments and slung his catapult at the giant. The stone hit him right in the middle of his forehead, cracking open his skull. Goliath crashed to the ground with a thump but that wasn't it for David. He still had one more gory deed to do.

You can find out what that is by reading Bible book 1 Samuel, chapter 17 and verses 51 to 54.

DEADLY DODGEMS

King Saul of Israel was getting fed up with everyone saying how great David (the lad who defeated Goliath) was. Because of his great courage the king had made David an officer in his army and everything he did seemed to go well. David's victory over Goliath and the Philistines had made him a hero and Saul was beginning to feel a bit over-shadowed by Israel's golden boy. In fact, the king was seething with jealousy. While David was playing his harp (was there no end to his talents?) King Saul tried to impale him with a spear. He threw his spear at David not once but twice, but the lad managed to dodge it just in the nick of time.

The king began to fear David because it was obvious that God was on his side. So Saul packed him off to battle again, probably hoping to get rid of him once and for all – and guess what? David had even more victories and became even more popular across Israel. Grrrrrrrrrrrrr!

King Saul was teeth-gnashingly furious that David was flavour of the month and he, the king, wasn't! In his jealousy he set about seeking to have David killed.

The king's son, Jonathan, discovered his dad's despicable plot and warned his best mate (David). Jonathan also tried to convince his dad that what he was doing was wrong. David was an innocent man and doing away with him would be a mega mistake. Saul finally calmed down and agreed to call off the death threat. Well, for a little while at least.

As soon as David had secured another victory in battle and his name was once again up in lights, all the anger and jealousy in Saul reawoke. Just like before, while David was strumming his harp for the king, Saul erupted and had another go at pinning his military hero to the palace wall. David dodged again and narrowly avoided a gory end.

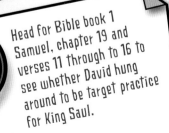

Head for Bible book 1 Samuel, chapter 19 and verses 11 through to 16 to see whether David hung around to be target practice for King Saul.

20
CATASTROPHIC COVER-UP

One thing you need to know about God is that He can see everything.

Nothing but nothing escapes His attention. So, when King David of Israel stepped out of line, God saw it all.

The Israelite army were off fighting and that's where the king should have been as well, heading up his troops. Instead, he was idling around his palace with far too much time on his hands for his own good.

One day he clapped eyes on a woman called Bathsheba as she went to take a bath. She was a real looker! David wanted the woman for himself and because he was the king he got what he wanted. Bathsheba fell pregnant with the king's child, but there was just one problem. She was already married to a fella called Uriah. David was in deep trouble and decided to try and cover his tracks by having Uriah brought back from the battlefield to make it look as if the baby was his. To King David's frustration Uriah wouldn't go anywhere near his wife. What was he to do to get himself off the hook?

David was beginning to get desperate when he hit upon another plan.

He had Uriah sent back to battle but made sure he was put in the front line. That way he'd be certain to be killed and with him off the scene, King David would be free to marry Bathsheba. And that's exactly what happened. Uriah met his gory end in a hail of arrows in the front line of battle. The king might have thought he'd got away with it but he hadn't. The Bible says that God was none too pleased with what David had done.

Look up Bible book 2 Samuel, chapter 12 and verses 15 to 19 to find out how this gory story ended.

21

A SLICE OF THE ACTION

Solomon was a fella from the Bible whose claim to fame was that he had 1,000 wives. Well, that was *one* of the things he was famous for.

He was also well known because he was so staggeringly rich he'd make most modern-day millionaires look as if they didn't have two pennies to rub together. Another thing he did was to build God a temple in Jerusalem (the capital city of Israel). All in all he was a pretty cool chap, but the secret of his success was not his wives or his wealth, but his wisdom.

When he took over as king from his dad (King David), Solomon figured that ruling God's special nation was a tall order, so he asked God for wisdom to help him do it. God came up with the goods and the rest is history – and it wasn't long before Solomon's amazing wisdom was put to the test.

Soon after Solomon's chat with God, a couple of ladies asked for an audience with the king. The story they had to tell made interesting listening and King Solomon was all ears. The long and the short of it was that both of them had given birth within a couple of days of each other. One of the women had supposedly rolled over on top of her baby while she was asleep and smothered it to death. When she realised the gruesome

horror of what she'd done she swapped the babies round. Sneaky! When the other woman woke up and found a dead baby beside her she took a closer look and soon discovered that it wasn't her kid at all. They'd been switched and she knew it. Solomon was going to need all the wisdom going to find out which of them was actually telling the truth.

While the two women argued it out before the king, Solomon came up with a brilliant solution to his dilemma. His suggestion was that if both of them reckoned the kid was theirs, then there was nothing for it but to cut the living baby in half and they could both have a half each. A bit gory, I suppose, but at least neither of them would lose out. Did that really happen?

Look up Bible book 1 Kings, chapter 3 and verses 26 through to 28 and find out for yourself.

YOU'VE BEEN FRAMED

King Ahab (of Israel) was a nasty piece of work but his wicked wife, Jezebel, beat him hands down when it came to being a baddy. Ahab might have been on Israel's throne but Jezebel pulled the strings. To prove my point, let me tell you the story of a man called Naboth.

Naboth owned a vineyard right by the king's palace. King Ahab fancied the idea of having a vegetable garden close to his palace and made Naboth an offer for his vineyard. Naboth could either have the cash or Ahab would find him a better vineyard elsewhere. Surely it was an offer he couldn't refuse. But he did. Naboth wasn't being awkward it was just that the vineyard had been in his family for generations and selling it simply wasn't an option.

Ahab slunk back home in a right old bad mood. He flung himself down on his bed and lay there in a big sulk. Jezebel tried to cajole him to get up and eat something but King Ahab wanted to stew in his juices. When he told his wife why he was feeling so depressed she came up with a cunning idea to get him Naboth's vineyard. Queen Jezebel was going to stitch Naboth up for something he hadn't done and then have him put to death. She rushed off some letters to the top bods in

Jezreel (where they lived) proclaiming a special day in honour of Naboth but told them also to round up a couple of rogues to accuse him of cursing God and her hubbie. And that's what happened. Naboth was publicly accused and taken away to be stoned to death.

With Naboth out of the way King Ahab wasted no time in getting his grubby hands on the dead man's vineyard. But God was having none of it and sent one of His top prophets (a guy called Elijah) to tell Ahab that in the place where dogs had licked up Naboth's blood, they would also lick up his.

Want to know whether that actually happened? Go to Bible book 1 Kings, chapter 22 and read verses 29 to 38.

'NOT FAIR!' PAIR

There are some things that God's really not too keen on and high up His list is grumbling and moaning. What's even worse is complaining about leaders. God hates that. So, when Moses' sister, Miriam, and elder brother, Aaron, started whingeing about Moses having a foreign (Cushite) wife, it didn't go down too well. The pair didn't stop there, either. There was something else that they weren't happy about.

Miriam was a prophetess and God sometimes spoke to the Israelites through her. Aaron had been Moses' right-hand man all the time they were rescuing the Israelites from slavery in Egypt. Why, then, was Moses the one who had the final say on things? Why was he top dog and not them? Why did everyone have to do what Moses said? Wasn't it about time that the pair of them had a bigger slice of the action? They were his brother and sister, after all, and who did he think he was anyway?

God wasn't prepared to discuss the matter with them there and then. Instead He arranged to meet the three of them at the tabernacle tent where sacrifices were made to Him. God showed up in a pillar of cloud at the entrance to the tent. Aaron and Miriam stepped forward and waited to hear what He had to say. God reminded them that, yes, He did speak to

the Israelites through people like them in dreams and visions, but that Moses was a different kettle of fish. He and Moses spoke face to face.

God was angry with Aaron and Miriam's grumbling attitude and, as He made His exit, Aaron looked across at his sister. Her skin was covered with a dreaded skin disease and was snow white. Aaron was scared and begged Moses not to let them be punished for what they'd said. He quickly realised that he and his sister had over-stepped the mark by criticising Moses, and he was well and truly sorry. Moses prayed to God to heal his sister even though she'd been in the wrong.

Take a look in Bible book Numbers, chapter 12 and verses 14 and 15 to see what became of Miriam.

24

A SHORT RULER

Zimri might not have been on Israel's throne for long but he certainly made his mark in the short time he was on the scene. It was a fella called Elah (son of Baasha) who was actually king of Israel at the time Zimri set his sights on taking over. Zimri was then an officer in the army and he was in charge of half the king's chariots. I guess he must have been getting a bit cheesed off with the same routine, day in day out, and that's why he figured he'd like to take a stab at king. In fact, that's exactly what he did!

King Elah was drinking himself silly at the house of one of the palace officials. While he was out for the count, Zimri seized the opportunity and killed him stone dead. Who knows how he managed it but the Bible tells us that Zimri took over as king. A bit of a big leap up the promotion ladder, I have to say, but he seemed to pull it off without any opposition.

Just to make sure it stayed that way, Zimri set about slaughtering Baasha's family. Every male relative and friend copped it. A clue as to how easy it had been for Zimri is that the Israelite army were out and about at the time battling with their enemies. When word got to them that Elah had been assassinated they picked a king of their own to rule them, their very own commander, Omri.

Israel's army hurried back to the city of Tirzah (where Zimri was acting as king) and attacked it. Zimri soon realised that his game was up and he was doomed. He went into the palace's inner fortress and set the palace on fire. And that's where Zimri met his gruesome end.

If you want to know how long (or rather, how short) Zimri ruled Israel for then flick through your Bible to 1 Kings, chapter 16 and verse 15.

25

PITY CITY

Hold on to your stomachs! This Bible story is *well* gory. The people of Samaria were holed up in their city by King Benhadad of Syria and his ruthless army. As the siege wore on, food supplies gradually ran out. The besieged Israelites resorted to eating anything they could lay their hands on. The Bible says that a donkey's head was going for eighty pieces of silver and two grammes of doves' dung cost five pieces of silver. Just in case that's put you off your dinner, doves' dung was probably another name for a type of vegetable.

Joram (king of Israel) was taking a stroll around the city when he was confronted by a hysterical woman. Joram presumed that she was begging for food. Not so! The woman had food all right, in fact that was the problem. She and another mum had decided that if they didn't want to die of starvation they'd have to eat their children. The woman cooked her son but when the time came to cook the other woman's kid, she'd gone and hidden him.

King Joram was distraught. What had it come to that his subjects were having to eat their kids to stay alive? He blamed the prophet, Elisha, for all of this, which seems a bit harsh, and sent out the order for him to be beheaded. Joram didn't much like what God had to say to him through Elisha and

wanted him out of his hair once and for all.

The good news is that when the king and his henchmen showed up at Elisha's place, the prophet of God managed to avoid the chop. He also had another message from God for the king. God was planning to come to the rescue of the Israelites and the proof was that there was gonna be food galore.

King Joram's personal attendant scoffed (sorry for the pun) at the very suggestion. Because of his lack of trust in God Elisha said that he'd see it happen but wouldn't get so much as a mouthful of the food. How did the fortunes of the inhabitants of Samaria turn around so quickly? Easy. God scared the living daylights out of the Syrians by making it sound as if they were being attacked by a ginormous army and they scarpered, leaving all their food behind.

Want to find out if what Elisha said to the king's assistant came true? Head for Bible book 2 Kings, chapter 7 and have a read of verses 16 through to 20.

26

SPLATTER-DAY!

Jezebel had been queen of Israel during the time that her hubbie (Ahab) had ruled as king. She was a nasty piece of work, in fact they both were.

After Ahab died, a couple of his sons (he actually had seventy in all!) had a shot at being king of Israel but they were both as bad as their dad.

First there was Ahaziah and then hot on his heels came Joram. God wasn't too happy with the hash they were making of ruling His special nation so He appointed His own choice of king (Jehu) to do the job instead.

Jehu was a good guy and he wanted Ahab's family (and the gods they worshipped) removed from the land. His first job was to get rid of King Joram. For your info, Joram's big brother (Ahaziah) was already dead. He'd met his end by falling from a balcony in his palace. Jehu climbed into his chariot and set off in hot pursuit of Joram. He wasted no time in finishing Joram off with an arrow that struck him in the back and punctured his heart. As if all this wasn't gory enough, Jehu still had one last score to settle. Yep, it was none other than Jezebel he was after.

Jezebel was living in Jezreel and she had no idea that her

number was up. While she was dolling herself up in the palace, Jehu thundered in on his chariot. Jezebel poked her head out of the window to see what all the commotion was, but Jehu wasn't going to waste his breath on her. He directed his attention towards Jezebel's officials and made them choose whose side they were on. Were they going to be loyal to their new king or to a queen who was about to meet her maker? It was a no-brainer.

Check out Bible book 2 Kings, chapter 9 and verses 32 to 37 to discover all the gory details of Jezebel's demise.

27

BYE BYE BAAL

There's nothing that God wants more than for the likes of you and me to get to know Him and to make Him number one in our lives. The Israelites were meant to be showing everyone else how to do this but often as not they failed miserably and ended up worshipping the gods of other nations instead. God was always giving the Israelites second chances to turn from their wicked ways, but He relied on their kings and leaders to bring about the change.

Jehu started out as a good king and was mega keen to rid Israel of anything and everything that displeased God, including the worship of the god, Baal. King Ahab (a few kings back) had given his backing to Baal worship but now King Jehu was planning to change that. Jehu had a cunning plan to kick Baal and his followers out of Israel once and for all. He made out that he was gonna serve Baal better than Ahab and arranged a big get-together for anybody who was a fan of this fake god. To make sure nobody slipped under the radar, Jehu threatened death for any Baal worshipper who didn't show up.

When the big day arrived, all the Baal bods were kitted out in sacred robes and ushered into the temple of Baal. Jehu did a double check that nobody who worshipped God had turned up by mistake. While eighty armed men hung around outside, Jehu kept up the act that he was big on Baal by offering sacrifices to the ghastly god. But that's where it ended. Jehu had had enough of playing games. It was time to finish what he'd started.

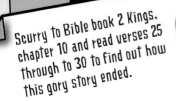

Scurry to Bible book 2 Kings, chapter 10 and read verses 25 through to 30 to find out how this gory story ended.

28

MEGA MIFFED MONARCH

One lesson the enemies of Israel quickly learned was that if you messed with Israel, you messed with God, and that certainly wasn't a smart move.

King Nahash of Ammon had been a loyal friend to David (Israel's king), so when he died, David was keen to tell the dead king's son, Hanun, how sorry he was and to return that loyalty. King David dispatched some messengers to convey his sympathies but when they arrived, a bunch of Ammonite leaders stirred up mischief and told Hanun (their new king) that they reckoned it was a trick and the men were Israelite spies.

More fool him, King Hanun believed their suspicious little minds and had the messengers seized, their beards shaved off, their clothes cut at the hips and they were sent packing back to King David. The poor fellas felt so ashamed that they *couldn't* go back, and they stayed in a place called Jericho while their beards grew again.

When news of their humiliation reached David's ears he was mega miffed. Oops! It looks as if King Hanun had made a bit of a boo-boo, and when he realised that for himself, he sent cartloads of silver to the Syrians to hire their army to protect the Ammonites from the wrath of King David.

The Israelite army made a beeline for Rabbah, the capital city of Ammon and got ready to attack it. The Ammonite army lined up at the entrance to their city and rent-an-army, from Syria, took up positions in the surrounding countryside. Joab (commander of the Israelite army) wasn't going to be outsmarted and split his army in two. His crack troops got ready to take on the Syrians and the rest of them prepared to give the Ammonites a walloping. The battle was over before it had begun. First to crumble under pressure were the Syrians who did a runner when Joab's men advanced. Then, when the Ammonites saw that all was lost they also retreated.

If you're wondering where the gory bit is in all of this then head for Bible book 1 Chronicles, chapter 19 and verses 16 to 19 to find out.

29

ZED DEAD

Zedekiah's claim to fame was that he was Judah's very last king. He was also quite young when he got the job (twenty-one) and he did his royal stuff for eleven years based in Jerusalem (Judah's capital city). For your info, Judah used to be part of Israel until there was a bit of a bust up and it split into two nations, Israel being one and Judah the other.

Zedekiah was what people call a 'puppet king' which meant that, although he sat on the throne, there was someone else more powerful pulling the strings and telling him what to do. That someone was none other than Mr Nasty himself, King Nebuchadnezzar of Babylon. The Babylonians had conquered Judah and poor Zed simply did what they said, or else!

Zedekiah eventually got cheesed off with being pushed around by Nebuchadnezzar and decided to rebel against his boss. Nasty Neb was having none of that. He rolled up at Jerusalem with a whopper of an army and laid siege to the place for over a year until its inhabitants were on the verge of starvation. King Zedekiah and his fighting men tried to make a run for it but the Babylonians caught up with them and overran the lot of 'em, capturing Judah's king in the process. Nebuchadnezzar was in no mood for mercy and had

Zedekiah's sons killed before his very eyes. That gruesome act was one of the last things Zedekiah ever saw (that's a clue) before Babylon's rotten riled ruler wrought revenge. (Try saying *that* quickly.)

If you want to find out how this gory story ends then you're going to need to hurry to Bible book Jeremiah, chapter 52 and verse 11.

30

DAN IS DEN DIN-DINS

Here's a Bible story I'll bet you've heard. It's about a guy called Daniel who was captured by the Babylonians (along with just about everyone else from his homeland of Judah) and taken away to live in far off Babylon. Daniel was just a teenager when he was exiled to Babylon but because God was on his case, he swiftly rose through the ranks of the Babylonian royal household and eventually ended up just one step away from being the country's main man. And that's where we catch up with Daniel in this Bible bit.

The king of Babylon (Darius) had elevated our Dan to the position of president (along with two other guys), ruling over the land's 120 governors. All was not sweetness and light between Daniel and the governors (or, for that matter, his two fellow presidents). They didn't like this social-climbing outsider one little bit and set about plotting his downfall. It was no secret that Daniel worshipped God so they tricked unsuspecting Darius into making it illegal to pray to anyone but their king for thirty days. Sneaky! Anyone caught disobeying this new law would be thrown into a den of lions. Did Daniel cave in to this devious decree? Nope! As bold as brass Daniel went home and prayed to God as if nothing had happened.

Daniel's enemies wasted no time in snitching him up to King Darius, who had no choice but to have his loyal servant arrested and flung into the lions' den. Darius was gutted that he'd been duped and he prayed that Daniel's God would protect him from becoming main course for those lunching lions. So, did Daniel turn into cat food or did Darius get his prayer answered?

All the gory details are revealed in Bible book Daniel, chapter 6 and verses 19 through to 24.

31

HORRID HEROD

The people of Israel were a patient lot. God had been telling them for hundreds of years that He was going to send someone really special to rescue them. Between you and me, most of them thought that this Messiah (the posh name for this special person) was going to rid the land of their Roman rulers, but no such luck. The sort of Messiah God was planning to send was someone who'd get their hearts right towards Him. Booting the Romans out of Israel was definitely not on His agenda. Anyway, after a long, long, long, long, long wait, word was finally out that a baby boy had been born somewhere in Israel who sounded as if He was the one God had been talking about.

Just to make sure the Israelites didn't miss the moment God let a bunch of stargazers from a distant land in on the news and sent them off in hot pursuit of the baby. If you're thinking that the fellas I'm talking about are those wise men from the Christmas story, you'd be spot on. They'd been following a rather helpful star that had led them all the way to Israel's capital city (Jerusalem). Better than sat nav any day!

The wise men fixed themselves an audience with Israel's wicked king, Herod, and explained that a star like the one they'd been following indicated that a new king had been born.

No surprises that Herod wasn't too impressed to discover that another king was on *his* patch.

After a bit of detective work Herod managed to find out that according to their holy scriptures, God's Messiah was going to be born in a little place called Bethlehem. Herod pretended that he'd also like to worship this new king and dispatched the wise men off to track down the baby.

Sure enough, they found Him (it was Jesus, if you hadn't guessed) and paid their respects to this special lad. Did they go back and tell Herod where he could find the boy? Certainly not. One of God's angels showed up and warned the men to go home another way, avoiding Jerusalem completely. When Herod found out that he'd been double-crossed he was livid.

To discover precisely how mega mad horrid Herod was check out Bible book Matthew, chapter 2 and verse 16.

32

SON DOWN

Every Easter, people remember the day that Jesus (God's Son) allowed Himself to be punished for all the bad stuff human beings have ever done. The thing is, however hard you try, it's just about impossible to get your head around what Jesus had to endure for the likes of you and me.

The story so far is that Jesus' enemies had got their way and made absolutely certain that Jesus had got the death sentence. They didn't like Him and the sooner He was out of the way the better was how they saw it.

Jesus had been well and truly stitched up (even though He was perfectly innocent) and handed over by His enemies to the Roman rulers of Israel to do their dirty work for them. Jesus was going to be executed by being nailed to a big wooden cross and then left to hang on it until He was dead.

The Roman soldiers were experts at this sort of thing and didn't need telling twice to lay into Jesus when He was handed over to them to be killed. Jesus was whipped, stripped and then had a crown made out of sharp thorns pressed onto His head to mock Him because of the claim that He was the King of the Jews. The Roman soldiers milked this for all it was worth and thought that pretending to worship Him as a king was a big joke. They beat Him, sneered at Him and spat at

Him, then led Him out to the place of execution.

To add insult to injury Jesus was forced to carry His own cross through the streets of Jerusalem to Golgotha, where He met His end. Was Jesus really God's one and only Son or did the fact that He suffered a gruesome death prove that He was powerless?

Flick to Bible book Matthew, chapter 27 and take a look at verses 45 through to 54 to read about the strange stuff that happened next and find your answer.

33

SWINE IS FINE

J esus and His disciples (the guys who hung around with Him) had just landed their fishing boat in a region called the Gadarenes after a pretty hairy time crossing the Sea of Galilee (which is actually a lake). Who knows whether the disciples were feeling a bit seasick after their stomach-turning voyage but there was no time to recuperate. As soon as Jesus and His followers set foot on dry land they were confronted by a mad man who lived in the tombs by the shore.

The poor man was in a terrible state. A bunch of evil spirits was making life an absolute misery for him and he was at his wits' end.

The reason he lived in the tombs was because he was out of his head and people couldn't cope with him living in the villages the way he was. They'd even tried to chain him up but he simply ripped the chains off with a super human strength. Day in, day out he would cry out in anguish and beat himself with rocks.

The man may not have had any idea who Jesus was but the evil spirits most certainly did. They were scared silly of Him because they knew that He was God and that He was going to call time on making a mess of this man's life. The evil spirits had what they thought was a brain wave. A herd of pigs was feeding on the nearby hillside. How about letting them go over and live in the pigs instead? Jesus agreed.

Want to find out the gory end to this unusual Bible story and also what became of the man? Read it all in Bible book Mark, chapter 5 and verses 13 to 20.

34

HEADS, YOU WIN

Poor John the Baptist was having a bit of a rough ride. He'd been locked up in prison by King Herod, Israel's rotten ruler. John was not one to mince words and he'd told Herod, point blank, that marrying his brother's wife (Herodias) was bang out of order. Between you and me, Herod was a tad scared of John. John (who was a prophet of God and a relative of Jesus) came across as a little bit crazy with his camel hair outfit and his weird appetite for locusts. Yuk! Herod did his level best to keep John out of harm's way just in case God held him responsible. As for Herodias, well, she wasn't fazed in the least by the funny fella. In fact, if she had her way he'd be history.

Things went pear-shaped for John when Herod decided to throw a party to celebrate his birthday. I'm guessing they didn't have discos in those days so when Herodias' daughter got up and danced for her uncle, the king, he was over the moon. The girl's party piece wowed Herod so much that he got a bit carried away and offered her anything she wanted (even up to half the kingdom!). Not bad for just a few minutes' work.

Herodias saw her chance and persuaded her daughter to ask for the head of John the Baptist. Gulp! Herod was flummoxed.

What was he to do? He couldn't go back on the promise he'd made to his niece in front of his party guests but the thought of killing John, the man of God, scared the pants off him. Herod's hands were tied and the order was given for John to be decapitated.

To find out how *not* to end a birthday party look up Bible book Mark, chapter 6 and verses 27 and 28.

35

TOMB RAIDER

'll be straight with you. This story's not as gory as it could have been if Jesus hadn't worked wonders and done some miracle-making stuff, but let's start at the beginning. Jesus was in Jerusalem (Israel's capital city) when news reached Him that His good buddy, Lazarus, was ill. Lazarus lived in Bethany which was only a short walk away (a couple of miles in fact). Jesus had healed oodles of people and He could have been at Lazarus' bedside in no time at all and restored His poorly pal. But that's not what Jesus did. He seemed to ignore the pleas of Mary and Martha (Lazarus' sisters) to heal their brother and stayed put in Jerusalem. What was He up to? Well, He did let slip a clue that something good was gonna come from this situation and that God would get the credit, but that didn't seem to be much help to ailing Lazarus.

Sure enough, two days later Jesus heard that Lazarus had died - and that's when He sprang into action. He headed off to Bethany with His disciples in tow. On His arrival He was met by a weeping and wailing Mary and Martha. They were distraught. They figured that if only Jesus had got there sooner then maybe their brother would still be alive. The Bible makes it clear that Jesus didn't find it easy seeing His good friends so upset, but He put His feelings on the back burner and made tracks for the tomb where the body of Lazarus had been laid. What was going on? You'll soon find out.

Jesus gave the order for the stone that covered the entrance to the tomb to be rolled away. Hang on a minute, was that a good idea? Martha pointed out to Jesus that her brother had been a gonner for four days. Surely Jesus wasn't thinking straight. Lazarus' body would be starting to rot and, being perfectly frank, it was going to smell something rotten.

Jesus reminded Martha what He'd said about God getting the credit for what was going to happen and stuck to His guns.

If you want to know whether Martha's fears were proved right check out Bible book John, chapter 11 and verses 41 through to 44.

36

DOUBLE TROUBLE

Until a couple of thousand years ago (or thereabouts) there wasn't such a thing as church. But after Jesus had returned to heaven He left a motley bunch of His mates in charge of continuing the work of showing people how they could get themselves back to being friends with God. When they began meeting together to worship God and to learn stuff about Him, 'church' is what they decided to call it. Church was the coolest place to be. People were getting healed by God, left, right and centre. God's love gushed out of everyone and they couldn't do enough to look after each other. The Bible says that there wasn't a needy person among the lot of 'em because those who had more stuff than they needed sold it and gave the proceeds to those who didn't.

That's what a guy called Ananias decided to do. He flogged a piece of property that he and his wife (Sapphira) owned and brought the cash to the leaders of the church. Actually, that's not completely accurate. Ananias didn't hand over all of the dosh. The sneaky hubbie and wife had agreed to hold back some of the money for themselves but to *pretend* that it was the whole amount. Whoops! Big mistake! God had told Peter (one of the church leaders) what the crooked couple

were up to. Peter confronted Ananias with his dodgy dealings and accused him not only of lying to them but worse still, of telling porky pies to God. No sooner had Peter spoken than Ananias keeled over and died.

Three hours later Sapphira showed up having no idea that her hubbie was dead and buried. Peter wanted to see whether she'd own up and come clean about the sale of their property. He quizzed her about how much money they'd made and Sapphira also lied to Peter's face.

Want to see if Ananias' wife also met a gory end? Then head for Bible book Acts, chapter 5 and read verses 9 to 11.

STONED DEAD

Being a Christian way back in the dim distant past when the Church was just kicking off was mega exciting, but it was also pretty risky. Not everyone liked what the Church was doing, particularly some of the Jewish religious leaders. They'd never been fans of Jesus when He'd been on the scene and they weren't any keener now on these followers of His who seemed to be converting people from their religion in droves. Something had to be done about them … and fast!

One of the Christians (a guy called Stephen) had really rubbed some of these religious people up the wrong way. Stephen was a leader in the Church and was doing great things for God. There seemed to be no stopping this dynamic deacon and when they tried to come against him with a war of words, Stephen's wisdom won the argument hands down.

If they couldn't beat this annoying fella fair and square in their religious debates then there was only one thing for it. They'd have to frame him. Stephen was accused by some lying witnesses of speaking against God (which was a crime in Jewish law) and put on trial. Was Stephen bothered? Not on your life. The Bible tells us that his face was like the face of an angel. Stephen put his confidence in God and wasn't going to be intimidated by any

religious lynch mob. He laid into his accusers with a history lesson about God and tried to show them that Jesus was the one their religion had been paving the way for.

Were they having any of it? No way! They didn't want a lecture from this follower of Jesus about how they'd got it wrong. Who did he think he was? When Stephen told them that they were just a bunch of stiff-necked people who got in God's way they were seething mad.

Did Stephen get let off with a warning for being so blunt? The answer is found in Bible book Acts, chapter 7 and verses 54 through to 60.

38

GORED 'GOD'

If there was one thing King Herod of Israel hated with a passion, it was Christians. In fact, such was his dislike of these followers of Jesus that there was nothing more pleasing to him than seeing them all dead. Herod targeted the leaders of the Christian Church with a vengeance and had one of them (James) put to death by the sword. Not nice! Many of the Jewish religious leaders shared Herod's hatred for the Christians and gave him a big thumbs up for killing James.

The king rather liked being popular so he thought he'd kill another big shot leader of the Church. His name was Peter. Herod had Peter flung into prison, but much to his annoyance one of God's angels rescued him. How inconvenient. King Herod was so cross that he had the prison guards executed. What a bloodthirsty story this is! But that's not the end of it. There's even more gore to come. Keep reading.

Some time later Herod had a falling out with the inhabitants of Tyre and Sidon. This wasn't a good thing for them because they relied upon the king for food. They figured it would be a smart move to make peace with Herod, and pretty sharpish at that. When King Herod made a state visit to their country they fell over backwards to suck up to him and to tell him what a swell fella he was. But when they cranked it up a gear and went as far as to call Herod a god, well, that's when things got just a little bit gory.

Head for Bible book Acts, chapter 12 and verse 23 to see how this callous king met his end.

39

FATAL FOLIAGE

Absalom was King David of Israel's favourite son but he'd got himself in a bit of a pickle by killing his elder brother, Amnon. He cleared off for three years until things between him and his dad were finally patched up. But they didn't stay like that for long. Absalom had his sights set on becoming Israel's next king, only things didn't seem to be going his way. If he couldn't get the throne by fair means then he'd have to take it by force. David's blue-eyed boy rebelled against his doting dad and rallied the nation to his side.

Now it was King David's turn to scarper. With just a small band of fighting men by his side, David fled the royal palace and headed for the hills. Before he scrammed, the king left spies in the city of Jerusalem (where the royal palace stood) to keep him informed of what Absalom was up to. One of the spies (Hushai) wangled his way into the court of Absalom and persuaded the prince to hold back from chasing after his dad and to prepare for a major attack instead. That bit of duff advice gave David extra time to get his army ready for war.

The long and the short of it was that when the two armies met in a forest (at a place called Ephraim) Absalom's fighting force was well and truly defeated. The battle was bloody and

around 20,000 men were slaughtered on that one day. But the forest was a dangerous place to fight and more people met their end because of that than were killed by the sword. David's son, Absalom, was one of them. He was riding his mule when he stumbled across his dad's servants. Absalom tried to escape but in the process rode under the bending branches of a big oak tree and got his head stuck. As he dangled in mid air the news of what had happened reached Joab (one of the king's commanders). King David had given orders that if Absalom was captured he wasn't to be killed. Did Joab do as he was told?

Read it all in Bible book 2 Samuel, chapter 18 and verses 14 and 15.

40
EAR TODAY, GONE TOMORROW

Here's a somewhat short gory story for you. Jesus knew that very soon He was going to be arrested and then handed over to the Romans to be executed. He'd done nothing to deserve it but this was all part of God's plan, and Jesus was prepared to obey His Father in heaven and go through with it.

Jesus and His disciples, the trusty trainees who went everywhere with Him, had shared one last meal together and were now making their way to a place called the Garden of Gethsemane. It was the dead of night and Jesus wanted some time alone to pray about what was going to happen to Him. While His disciples dozed in the olive grove Jesus agonised over what awaited Him the next day. He wasn't too pleased that His friends couldn't even stay awake to give Him some moral support. This was not an easy time.

At that moment a menacing mob appeared. They'd come to arrest Jesus armed with swords and clubs. Jesus stood His ground and waited for them to make the first move. But Peter, one of Jesus' disciples, was having none of it. Hot-headed Pete wasn't going to let anyone lay their hands on his Master. He pulled out his sword and sliced off the ear of one of the mob. Gruesome or what? But that's not how this story ends.

Check out Bible book Luke, chapter 22 and verse 51 for an unusually happy ending to a gory Bible story.

41

BONE BATTLE

For a few hundred years of its history the land of Israel had people called 'judges' running the show as its leaders. One of them was a chap you might well have come across. He was called Samson and he was famous for his amazing, super duper, God-given strength. The Philistines were neighbours of the Israelites and they were forever at each other's throats fighting about one thing or another. Samson was a bit of a hothead himself and he didn't need much persuading to take on the Philistines single-handed. There was nothing he liked more than a good old scrap with them. For their part, the Philistines reckoned that if only they could get rid of Samson once and for all, life would be a lot easier. So that's precisely what they decided to do.

The Philistines set up camp near the Israelites and attacked a town called Lehi in the hope of capturing that nuisance, Samson. The Israelites weren't in the mood for a fight with the Philistines and went in search of their strongman so that they could hand him over to the enemy. Samson convinced his countrymen not to kill him but to tie him up and give him to the Philistines, which they did.

The Philistines were well chuffed when they saw that

Samson was bound up and ready for the taking. But before they could lay their hands on him, God's Spirit came upon Israel's mighty man and he burst out of his bonds as if they were made of paper. Nothing could stop him now. Samson was champing at the bit for a fight. He clapped his eyes on an ass's jaw-bone and made a grab for it.

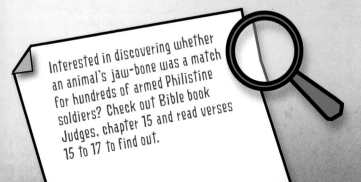

Interested in discovering whether an animal's jaw-bone was a match for hundreds of armed Philistine soldiers? Check out Bible book Judges, chapter 15 and read verses 15 to 17 to find out.

42
NIGHT STRIKE

Moses had tried just about everything he could to persuade Pharaoh to obey God and set his Israelite slaves free, but Egypt's king was having none of it. God had sent one plague after another to show Pharaoh who was boss but nothing doing. Pharaoh wasn't gonna budge. In the end, God was left with no alternative but to inflict one final punishment on the Egyptians. He was planning to kill every oldest son and every first-born creature in Egypt. Maybe then stubborn Pharaoh would realise that you don't mess with God.

But first things first. God had some important instructions to give the Hebrews to make sure that they weren't touched by His punishment. They were told that when God gave them the go ahead to they were kill a goat or a lamb and to daub its blood all around their front doors. The meat was then to be eaten as part of a special meal that would help the Israelites remember what God was going to do for them. There were other things, too, that God told the Israelites to do during the build up to the time when He was going to set them free. Finally the big day arrived and the Israelites shut themselves indoors and waited for Him to do His stuff.

At around midnight God showed up. He passed right over the Hebrew homes where the door-frames were splattered with blood, but the Egyptians weren't so lucky. God struck down every first-born male in the land. It was horrendous. There was weeping and wailing from one end of Egypt to the other.

Did God's gory punishment do the trick or did Pharaoh dig his stubborn heels in even further? Find out in Bible book Exodus, chapter 12 and verse 31.

43
SUPER-SIZED SACRIFICE

I f you didn't know it already, let me be the first to tell you that the Bible is divided into two parts. There's what's called the Old Testament (which is all to do with stuff before Jesus was born) and then there's the New Testament which kicks off with the birth of Jesus and goes on from there. The Old Testament bit of the Bible is the place where you can read all about animals being sacrificed to God (if that's what you enjoy!).

Why *were* animals sacrificed? A good question. To cut a long story short, animals were killed by a bunch of Israelites (called priests) as a way of reminding the people they needed forgiveness from God for the wrong things they'd done. That's it in a nutshell. Being a priest was sort of a cross between a butcher and a vicar. One thing's for certain, it was a messy old business. All of this went on in a special tent called the tabernacle which travelled with the Israelites wherever they went.

After traipsing around for years in the desert the Israelites eventually put down roots in the land of Canaan. One of their kings (David) thought it would be a brill idea to build a permanent tabernacle but it took his son (Solomon) to get round to sorting it. The building would go by the name of the 'Temple' and King Solomon spared absolutely no expense in making it a place fit for God. Between you and me it was God who'd supplied the blueprints for the Temple in the first place so no wonder it was impressive. According to the Bible it took 210,000 men seven whole years to build. Wow!

When the time came for the Temple to be officially opened, King Solomon laid on the most lavish dedication ceremony you could ever imagine. If you want to read about the goriest part of that special day and to find out how many animals were slaughtered I'll let you do your own detective work.

Head for Bible book 1 Kings, chapter 8 and verses 62 to 63 for the gory facts.

44

JAMMY JOASH

The nation of Israel had been split into two kingdoms. There was Judah (which by and large worshipped God) and then there was Israel (which by and large didn't). Queen Athalia was the daughter of Israel's wicked king, Ahab, and his equally wicked wife, Jezebel, but she'd gone and got married to King Jehoram of Judah which made things a tad more complicated. The pair of them tried to patch things up between the two kingdoms, but because Israel didn't worship God (they worshipped the god Baal), it didn't really work. When King Jehoram died, his son, Ahaziah, took over. Athalia (his mum) seized the opportunity and used her power and influence to establish the worship of the god Baal in Judah in a big way.

Unfortunately, King Ahaziah's reign was cut short when he was assassinated after just a year on the throne, and that left Athalia in charge of Judah. Top of the wicked queen's priority list was to kill off the royal family of Judah which included Ahaziah's son, Joash.

Just in the nick of time Joash was rescued by his aunt (Jehosheba) and whisked away to safety. She hid him and his nurse in a bedroom at the Temple of God and they lived there

in secret and out of harm's way. A priest called Jehoiada was in on this and at the end of six years he set about getting rid of Judah's quirky queen and installing Joash as the rightful king.

Jehoiada had Ahaziah's son brought out from his place of hiding and surrounded by a massive armed guard for his protection. Joash was led to the front of the Temple and proclaimed king of Judah by the brave priest. It was obviously a popular decision because the Bible says that the crowd cheered and clapped. When Queen Athalia heard the commotion she went to investigate. Joash, as Judah's newly-crowned king, was standing at the entrance to the Temple, surrounded by officers, guards, trumpeters and an adoring crowd of onlookers. Athalia was furious and tore her clothes to prove the point.

To see what happened next check out Bible book 2 Kings, chapter 11 and read verses 15 and 16.

45

ROCKY REVENGE

The kingdom of Judah had loads and loads of kings and one of its better ones (for most of the time) was Amaziah. He was just twenty-five when he took up this top job and did his very best to do things God's way, if somewhat reluctantly. First off he executed the officials who'd murdered his dad, Joash, the previous king of Judah. Next he set about attacking the rebellious Edomites and bringing them into submission once more.

King Amaziah didn't do things by halves and rallied 3,000 men of fighting age (over twenty years old) to wage war. They were organised into units of hundreds and thousands with officers in charge of them.

As if that wasn't enough soldiers to win a war, Amaziah roped in a whopping extra 100,000 soldiers from nearby Israel. But this wasn't a good move and God had something to say about it. Unlike the people of Judah, at that time the Israelites didn't worship God and He wasn't planning to give His support to anything that involved them. God told the king (through a prophet) that although he might think that adding the Israelites to his army would make it stronger, he was wrong, wrong, wrong! Go with them and God would

allow the Edomites to defeat Judah's army. But go without them and God would make up the difference and give Judah the victory.

Amaziah was in a bit of a quandary. He'd gone and forked out a cool 3,400 kilogrammes of silver to hire the Israelite troops (and that was a lot of dosh) and now it would be for nothing. God assured the king that it was easy peasy for Him to give Amaziah loads more than that any time He wanted. It wasn't a problem. So, although they weren't too happy about it, the Israelite soldiers were sent home.

Meanwhile, King Amaziah summoned up his courage and went off with his army to do battle with the Edomites. Sure enough, with God on their side they had the upper hand and slaughtered 10,000 of their enemies.

They also captured as many prisoners but to discover their fate you'll need to read up Bible book 2 Chronicles, chapter 25 and verse 12.

46

TOO BIG FOR HIS BOOTS

Uzziah was just sixteen when he became king of Judah and he stuck with it for an amazing fifty-two years. Not bad going, eh? He followed in the footsteps of his dad (King Amaziah) and tried to live a life that pleased God. The Bible says that credit must go to Uzziah's religious adviser (Zedekiah) for keeping the young king on the straight and narrow. God blessed King Uzziah, big time, because he put God first.

The surrounding countries were at war with Judah most of the time. Judah's inhabitants worshipped God but none of the other nations did and that alone caused loads of friction. King Uzziah (with God's help) fought against the lot of 'em and beat them every time. He became so powerful and respected that his fame even spread to far away Egypt. He also spent his energies on strengthening the fortifications of Jerusalem (Judah's capital) and, because he loved farming, encouraged his people to plant vineyards and to work the fertile land.

The king's army was massive (over 300,000) and they had the best equipment going. He even had boffins designing weird and wonderful gadgets to catapult large boulders over the city wall and for shooting flaming arrows at the enemy.

Life was great with Uzziah at the helm. But then things changed. It seemed as if all this great power had gone to his head and the king became proud and arrogant.

He really lost it when he went into God's Temple and burned some incense to God on the altar. What's wrong with that, you may ask? I'll tell you. The job of doing that was down to some guys called priests. They'd been specially prepared (or consecrated) to go into the Temple to do this job. For everyone else (including King Uzziah) the place was out of bounds. The priests confronted Uzziah but he wasn't going to be pushed around by anybody. God was not impressed.

Want to know what gory punishment the king got for stepping over the line? Head for Bible book 2 Chronicles, chapter 26 and verses 19 to 21.

47

DOOM AND DESTRUCTION

The very last book of the Bible (it's called Revelation) has got loads of gory stuff in it, but we've just handpicked some of the best bits for you to get your teeth into. A big chunk of this Bible book is all about what's going to happen way off in the future, and it fills us in with how God's gonna deal with all the people who have turned their backs on Him. We get a behind-the-scenes view of things from God's HQ in heaven, and we catch up with the story as a bunch of angels (with trumpets) have been given the go ahead by God to do some damage to all the stiff-necked bad guys who've ruined the world. Four of the angels have already got stuck in and wiped loads and loads of people off the face of the earth, and now it's time for Angel Number 5 to step up to the plate.

Angel Number 5 blasted his trumpet and a dark, bottomless pit was unlocked, letting loose swarms of locusts. These weren't your typical sort of locust. These were mean machines with scorpion-like power to attack and torture God's enemies. To make things worse, when people got stung by their vicious tails it didn't kill them. Instead they had to live with the terrible pain for months and months, wishing they could die but not being able to.

Next up was Angel Number 6 and with a blast from his trumpet, hundreds of thousands of warriors on horseback were released to wreak havoc on the earth. Fire, smoke and sulphur poured out of the horses' mouths as they slaughtered a third of the world's population. Now, I don't know about you, but after all that destruction I think I'd get the message that God wasn't too pleased with the way I was behaving and I reckon I'd be in a bit of a hurry to mend my wicked ways. Want to find out what the survivors of these gory punishments did?

Check out Bible book Revelation, chapter 9 and look up verses 20 and 21 for your answer.

48
DOUBLE-MINDED DISCIPLES

Jesus (and a couple of His best buddies) were on their way back from a bit of a wild mountain meeting with God. On their journey down, they came across the rest of Jesus' gang who were having a bit of a hard time with some religious leaders and a rowdy crowd of onlookers. The disciples had been trying their level best to heal a boy who was suffering from fits and seizures but without any success. The poor kid was rolling around on the ground, foaming at the mouth and gnashing his teeth. The boy's dad was at his wits' end and told Jesus that he'd asked the disciples to set his son free from the evil spirit that was behind all this, but they couldn't come up with the goods.

Jesus wasn't a happy bunny. The whole point of being His disciples was so that they could watch what He was doing and then do it for themselves. The trouble was that they still hadn't quite got what it meant to have faith in God. All Jesus was expecting from them was to trust in God 100 per cent and the boy would have been set free. But that wasn't going to happen until they stopped mixing their trust in God with a load of unhelpful thoughts about all the reasons why the boy might not get healed.

Jesus had had enough of this time-wasting and took control of the situation. The boy's dad begged Him to do something, if it was at all possible. Jesus wasn't standing for any of that 'if you can' nonsense. He told the man that God could do absolutely anything. All he had to do was believe it. And with that, Jesus took the bull by the horns and told the evil spirit that was causing all the trouble to leave the lad.

Want to find out if this story has a happy ending? Head for Bible book Mark, chapter 9 and verses 26 and 27 where all is revealed.

49 KINGDOM KIDS

T his Bible bit might be a teensy one but it packs a big
punch. Jesus had been chatting to His disciples about
God's kingdom. For your info, God's kingdom isn't
an actual place like America, Britain or Africa, it's simply
anywhere where God is allowed to be in charge. If God is
number one in your life then you're in God's kingdom, end
of story. Jesus' disciples had a bit of a puzzler for Jesus. They
wanted to know who was the greatest in God's kingdom.
Were they hoping Jesus would say it was them? Who knows?

Jesus answered their question in a round about sort of way.
He plonked a child in the middle of them and said that unless
they became like kids then no way would they get within a
million miles of God's kingdom. Well, Jesus didn't quite use
those words but it's more or less what He meant. The point
He was making was that children are far more trusting than
most grown ups and for God to be the main man in your life,
you've gotta be humble and not proud. You've gotta trust in
God and not in how great you think you are.

That wasn't the end of it. Jesus warned the disciples that
anyone who deliberately caused a kid to go off the rails was
going to get their come-uppance from God.

Jesus didn't stop at that either. He had some more heavy (and gory) stuff to say about people who do bad things. Look up Bible book Matthew, chapter 18 and verses 8 and 9.

FIERY FINALE

If you're a fan of musicals you'll know that most of them have a big finale so that the show ends with a bang. Well, that's sort of how the Bible rounds up in Bible book Revelation. All through the Bible there are stories about people who won't have anything to do with God and think nothing of killing those who worship Him. Not only that, but God's also got an invisible enemy (well, he's invisible to you and me – God can see him). He's called the devil (or Satan) and he's the mastermind behind all the bad stuff that goes on in the world.

The Bible tells us that there's gonna come a day when God's enemies (and that includes Satan) have one last shot at trying to get rid of God. It's a really gory story and it begins with Jesus riding out of heaven as a mighty warrior at the head of an awesome angel army. What are God's enemies thinking? There's no way that they're going to get one over on God. Sure enough the lot of them get wiped out, every last man. Two of the worst culprits are flung into a lake of fire. The rest are slaughtered by the sword and then their bodies get eaten up by a ginormous flock of birds.

The gory stuff doesn't quite end there. God has one more

score to settle. Satan was the one who was there at the beginning of the world and messed things up between God and human beings. Now it's time to end his reckless reign of terror. Satan is chucked into a scorching lake of fire and sulphur where he gets tormented forever and ever.

This gory story actually has a happy ending – well, it does for everyone who loves God.

Have a read of Bible book Revelation, chapter 21 and verses 1 through to 4 to find out a good reason for making sure you get to know God.

NATIONAL DISTRIBUTORS

UK: (and countries not listed below)
CWR, Waverley Abbey House, Waverley Lane, Farnham, Surrey GU9 8EP.
Tel: (01252) 784700 Outside UK (44) 1252 784700 Email: mail@cwr.org.uk

AUSTRALIA: KI Entertainment, Unit 21 317-321 Woodpark Road, Smithfield,
New South Wales 2164. Tel: 1 800 850 777 Fax: 02 9604 3699
Email: sales@kientertainment.com.au

CANADA: David C Cook Distribution Canada, PO Box 98, 55 Woodslee Avenue,
Paris, Ontario N3L 3E5. Tel: 1800 263 2664 Email: joy.kearley@davidccook.ca

GHANA: Challenge Enterprises of Ghana, PO Box 5723, Accra
Tel: (021) 222437/223249 Fax: (021) 226227 Email: ceg@africaonline.com.gh

HONG KONG: Cross Communications Ltd, 11/F Ko's House, 577 Nathan Road,
Kowloon. Tel: 2780 1188 Fax: 2770 6229 Email: cross@crosshk.com

INDIA: Crystal Communications, Plot No. 125, Road No. 7, T.M.C, Mahendra Hills,
East Marredpally, Secunderabad - 500026. Tel/Fax: (040) 27737145
Email: crystal_edwj@rediffmail.com

KENYA: Keswick Books and Gifts Ltd, PO Box 10242-00400, Nairobi
Tel: (020) 2226047/312639 Email: sales.keswick@africaonline.co.ke

MALAYSIA: Canaanland Distributors Sdn Bhd, No. 25 Jalan PJU 1A/41B, NZX
Commercial Centre, Ara Jaya, 47301 Petaling Jaya, Selangor. Tel: (03) 7885 0540/1/2
Fax: (03) 7885 0545 Email: info@canaanland.com.my

Salvation Publishing & Distribution Sdn Bhd, 23 Jalan SS 2/64, 47300 Petaling Jaya,
Selangor. Tel: (03) 78766411/78766797 Fax: (03) 78757066/78756360 Email: info@
salvationbookcentre.com

NEW ZEALAND: KI Entertainment, Unit 21 317-321 Woodpark Road, Smithfield,
New South Wales 2164, Australia. Tel: 0 800 850 777 Fax: +612 9604 3699
Email: sales@kientertainment.com.au

NIGERIA: FBFM, Helen Baugh House, 96 St Finbarr's College Road, Akoka, Lagos
Tel: (+234) 01-7747429, 08075201777, 08186337699, 08154453905
Email: fbfm_1@yahoo.com

PHILIPPINES: OMF Literature Inc, 776 Boni Avenue, Mandaluyong City
Tel: (02) 531 2183 Fax: (02) 531 1960 Email: gloadlaon@omflit.com

SINGAPORE: Alby Commercial Enterprises Pte Ltd, 95 Kallang Avenue #04-00,
AIS Industrial Building, 339420. Tel: (+65) 629 27238 Fax: (+65) 629 27235
Email: marketing@alby.com.sg

SOUTH AFRICA: Life Media & Distribution, Unit 20, Tungesten Industrial Park, 7
C R Swart Drive, Strydompark 2125. Tel: (+27) 0117924277 Fax: (+27) 0117924512
Email: orders@lifemedia.co.za

SRI LANKA: Christombu Publications (Pvt) Ltd, Bartleet House, 65 Braybrooke
Place, Colombo 2. Tel: (+941) 2421073/2447665
Email: christombupublications@gmail.com

USA: David C Cook Distribution Canada, PO Box 98, 55 Woodslee Avenue, Paris,
Ontario N3L 3E5, Canada. Tel: 1800 263 2664 Email: joy.kearley@davidccook.ca

CWR is a Registered Charity – Number 294387
CWR is a Limited Company registered in England – Registration Number 1990308

More of Andy Robb's colourful Bible stories with crazy cartoons and cliff-hanger endings, to stop you getting bored!

50 Weirdest Bible Stories

Discover fifty of the weirdest things that happened in the Bible including the crossing of the Red Sea, Jesus healing a paralysed man, heavenly bread in the desert, the strange dreams of Joseph, Peter walking on water and many more. Want some weirdness? Go for it!

ISBN: 978-1-85345-489-9

50 Wildest Bible Stories

A slippery serpent suggested sin, a bunch of builders babbled away, a pair of past-it parents produced a baby, angels ate with a guy called Abe, bad boys became bear bait! Looking for a really wild time? Tuck in!

ISBN: 978-1-85345-529-2

50 Craziest Bible Stories

Some crazy things happened in the Bible like the stories of Jonah and the big fish, Elijah and the prophets of Baal, Balaam and the donkey, the feeding of the 5,000, and Jesus' resurrection.
Go on – get ka-rayzee!

ISBN: 978-1-85345-490-5

50 Wackiest Bible Stories

A nine-foot giant, big fish travel, getting a drink out of a rock, the right and wrong ways to carry a box the size of a coffee table – these are just a few of the stories that you can enjoy between the covers of this very wacky book.

ISBN: 978-1-85345-983-2

50 Juiciest Bible Stories

Crop-destroying locusts, body-covering boils, ventriloquists, disappearing people, shipwrecks, wonder wives, scheming fathers, feuding families and a Tip Top Tent – lots of unusual things happened in Bible times! So what are you waiting for? Leap in!

ISBN: 978-1-85345-984-9

50 Barmiest Bible Stories

A prophet who became a bear's lunch, a king with a whopping 1,000 wives to keep happy, a bunch of rebels who were zapped by fire from heaven ... plenty of totally barmy things went on in Bible times! In this book you'll find fifty of the barmiest!

ISBN: 978-1-85345-852-1

For current prices visit **www.cwr.org.uk**

MORE FROM ANDY ROBB

Professor Bumblebrain offers some exciting explanations, colourful cartoons and (ahem) 'hilarious' jokes answering these important questions:

Who is God? What is He like?
Where does He live?
How can I get to know Him?
ISBN: 978-1-85345-579-7

Who's the bravest? Who's the funniest? Who's the jammiest?
Who's the strongest?
ISBN: 978-1-85345-578-0

Who is Jesus? Where did He come from? What was His mission? What's it to me?
ISBN: 978-1-85345-623-7

Who made the universe?
How old is planet earth?
What about dinosaurs?
Was there really a worldwide flood?
ISBN: 978-1-85345-622-0

Learn about the meaning behind The Prodigal Son, The Wise and Foolish Man, The Lost Sheep and many more!
ISBN: 978-1-85345-947-4

What is prayer? How can we use it? Does it work? Who in the Bible used it?
ISBN: 978-1-85345-948-1

Dig deeper into God's Word

In each issue the Topz Gang teach you biblical truths through word games, puzzles, riddles, cartoons, competitions, simple prayers and daily Bible readings.

Available as individual issues or annual subscription. For current prices and to order visit **www.cwr.org.uk/topzeveryday**

Never did reading the Bible look so good! Get eye-opening, jaw-dropping Bible readings and notes every day, plus special features and articles in every issue (covers two months).

Available as individual issues or annual subscription. For current prices and to order visit **www.cwr.org.uk/youth**

TOPZ SECRET STORIES
from Alexa Tewkesbury

The Topz Secret Stories are full of fun as they help you discover things about yourselves and God. They include humour, relevance and spiritual insight as the rival Dixons gang present problems and opportunities to the Topz gang.

Danny and the Runaway
ISBN: 978-1-85345-991-7

The Cloudgate Mystery
ISBN: 978-1-85345-992-4

One Too Many For Benny
ISBN: 978-1-85345-915-3

Pantomime Pandemonium
ISBN: 978-1-85345-916-0

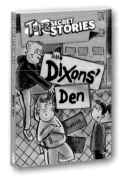

Dixon's Den
ISBN: 978-1-85345-690-9

Dixon's and the Wolf
ISBN: 978-1-85345-691-6

For current prices, visit **www.cwr.org.uk/store**
Available online or from Christian bookshops.